01 PRE-SHOOT CHECKLIST

Check these settings before you head out with your camera!

SETTING	MY PREFERRED SETTING
☑ Shooting Mode	....
☑ ISO	....
☑ White Balance	....
☑ Focus Mode	....
☑ Focus Target	....
☑ Drive Mode	....
☑ Metering Mode	....
☑ Bracketing On/Off	....
☑ Image Quality and Size	....
☑ Image Stabilization	....
☑ Flash Mode	....
☑ Picture Mode	....
☑ Exposure Compensation	....
☑ Battery Fully Charged and In Camera	....
☑ Memory Card Formatted and In Camera	....

02 BUTTONS, DIALS, AND SCREENS

CAMERA BODY TOP

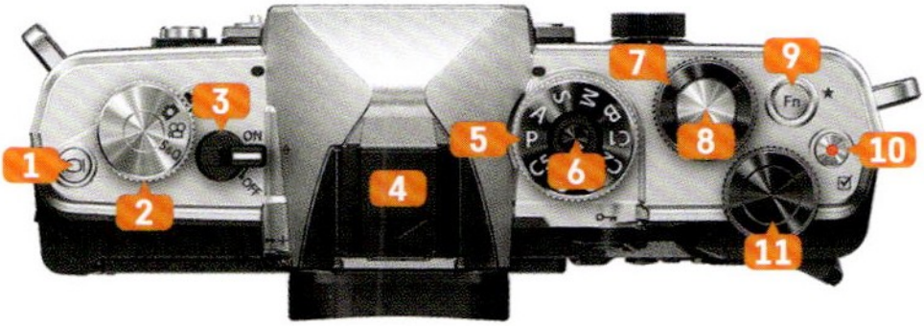

1. **Live View (LV) Button:** Use to switch between the live view and the super control panel view on the monitor.
2. **Photos/Movies/Slow & Quick Mode (S&Q) Dial:** Switch between shooting still photos, movies, and slow motion/fast motion movies. When in movie or S&Q mode, rotate the front dial to choose the exposure mode (P, A, S, M). In S&Q mode, movies can be recorded for sensor frame rates different from the playback frame rate. No sound is recorded in S&Q mode.
3. **On/Off Lever:** Turns the camera on and off.
4. **Hot Shoe:** External flash unit mounts here.
5. **Mode Dial:** Use to select the shooting mode.
6. **Mode Dial Lock Button:** Press to lock/unlock the mode dial.
7. **Front Dial:** Controls functions on the camera depending on the mode.
8. **Shutter Button:** Press halfway down to activate autofocus and all the way down to take the photo.

9. Function (Fn) Button: Default is to control exposure compensation.
10. Movie Button/Selection Button: Use to start/stop movie recording/Used for selecting images during Playback.
11. Rear Dial: Controls functions on the camera depending on the mode.

CAMERA BODY FRONT

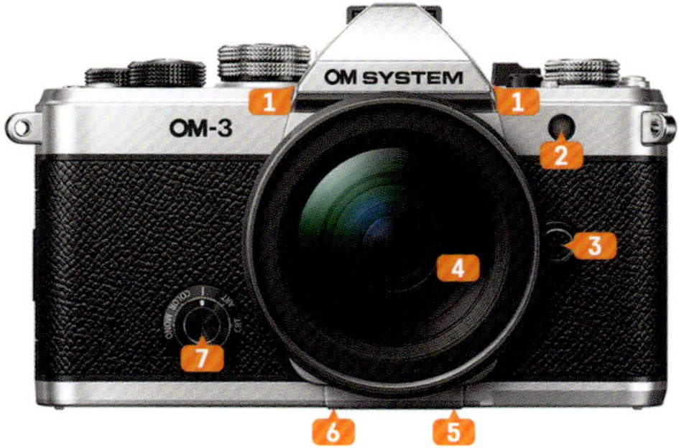

1. Stereo Microphones: Records audio when shooting movies.
2. Self-Timer Lamp/AF Illuminator/Movie Recording Lamp: Lights up and blinks when using self-timer/Helps autofocus in low light/ Lights up when recording movies.
3. Lens Release Button: Push button, then turn the lens to remove it from the camera.
4. Micro Four Thirds (4:3) Imaging Sensor (behind lens): The camera's 20.4-megapixel sensor.
5. Battery Compartment (on bottom): Where the camera battery goes.
6. Tripod Socket (on bottom): Used to attach a tripod or monopod.
7. Creative Dial: See Chapter 04.

CAMERA BODY BACK

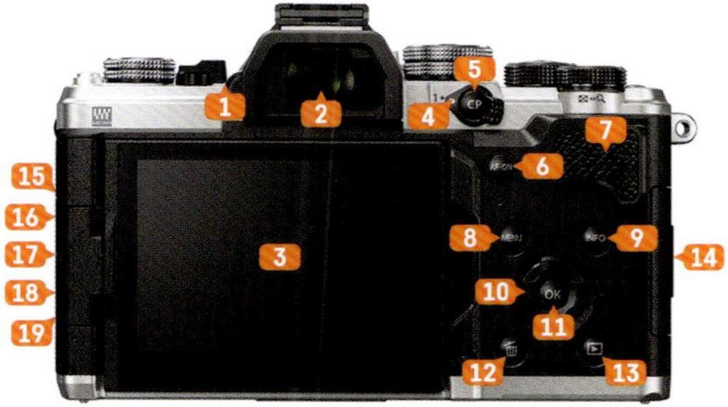

1. **Diopter Adjustment Dial:** Use to focus the viewfinder display.
2. **Electronic Viewfinder:** The viewfinder.
3. **LCD Monitor Touchscreen:** Monitor and touchscreen.
4. **Fn Lever:** Use Menu > Custom Menu > 1. Operations > Fn Lever Function to set up.
5. **CP/PROTECT Button:** Press the CP (Computational Photography) button and rotate the front or rear dial to pick a Computational Mode or setting/Used during image playback to protect an image from deletion.
6. **AF-ON Button:** Activates autofocus.
7. **Speaker:** Used to play sound during movie playback.
8. **Menu Button:** Opens and closes camera menu system.
9. **INFO Button:** Use to cycle through information screens.
10. **Arrow Keypad Buttons:** Use to move the focus target and navigate menu items.
11. **OK Button:** Use in camera menu operations. Press to open the super control panel.

12. **Erase Button:** Use to delete the current image on the monitor.
13. **Playback Button:** Press to review images on the monitor.
14. **Memory Cards Slot (under cover on side):** There is one SD/SDHC/SDXC memory card slot.
15. **Microphone Connector (on side):** 3.5mm stereo minijack to connect an external microphone.
16. **Headphone Connector (on side):** 3.5mm stereo minijack to connect headphones.
17. **HDMI Connector (Type D) (on side):** Use to connect HDMI Micro (type D) cable.
18. **USB Connector (Type C) (on side):** Use to connect USB type C cable.
19. **Rubber Cover (on side):** Protects connectors.

VIEWFINDER/LIVE VIEW SCREEN

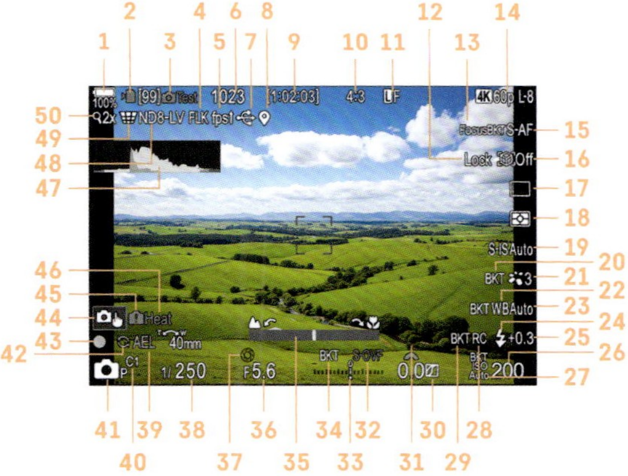

1. Battery Level
2. Card Write Indicator
3. Test Photo
4. Anti-Flicker Shooting
5. Frame Rate
6. Number of Storable Still Photos
7. Active USB Connection
8. Bluetooth Position Information
9. Available Movie Recording Time
10. Aspect Ratio
11. Image Quality
12. Subject Selection Lock
13. Focus Bracketing
14. Movie Quality

15. AF Mode
16. Subject Detection
17. Drive Mode
18. Metering Mode
19. Image Stabilizer
20. ART Bracket
21. Picture Mode
22. WB Bracketing
23. White Balance
24. Flash Mode
25. Flash Intensity Control
26. ISO
27. ISO Bracketing
28. RC Mode
29. Flash Bracketing
30. Highlight and Shadow Control
31. Exposure Compensation Value
32. LV Settings
33. Exposure Compensation
34. AE Bracketing
35. Focus Indicator
36. Aperture Value
37. Depth of Field Preview
38. Shutter Speed
39. AE Lock
40. Custom Mode
41. Shooting Mode
42. Pro Capture Active
43. AF Confirmation Mark
44. Touch Operation
45. Internal Temperature Warning
46. Lens Focal Length/Zoom Operation
47. Histogram
48. Live ND Shooting
49. Keystone Compensation
50. Digital Tele-Converter

SUPER CONTROL PANEL/LIVE VIEW

SUPER CONTROL PANEL

The super control panel/LV super control panel allows quick access to the following settings. Press the OK button, then use the arrow keypad (or just tap on the screen) to select the setting. Use the front and rear dials to change the setting, then press the shutter button halfway down to save the current settings and exit.

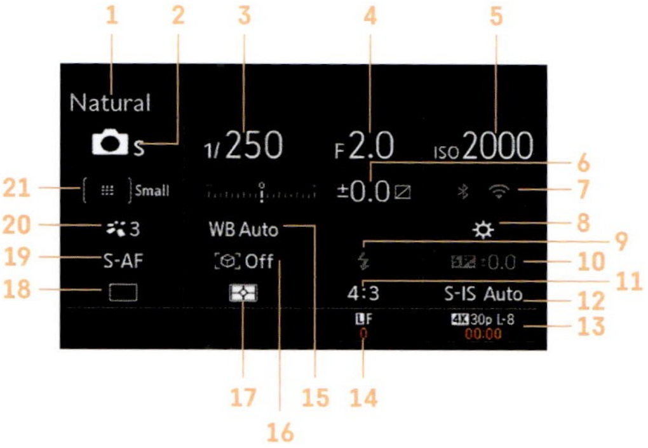

1. Currently Selected Option
2. Shooting Mode
3. Shutter Speed
4. Aperture
5. ISO
6. Exposure Compensation Value
7. Wi-Fi/Bluetooth
8. Button Function
9. Flash Mode
10. Flash Intensity Control
11. Aspect Ratio
12. Image-Stabilizer
13. Movie Quality/Available Recording Time
14. Image Quality/Number of Storable Images
15. White Balance/Color Temperature
16. Subject Detection
17. Metering Mode
18. Drive Mode
19. AF Mode
20. Picture Mode
21. AF Target

03 ESSENTIAL MODES AND SETTINGS

SHOOTING MODES

Press the mode dial lock button down to unlock the mode dial, then turn the dial to the desired shooting mode. Press the mode dial lock button a second time to lock in your selection.

P (Program): The camera sets the shutter speed and aperture based on metering info and current ISO.

A (Aperture Priority): You set the aperture, and the camera sets the shutter speed based on metering info and current ISO. Range of available apertures depends on the attached lens.

S (Shutter Speed Priority): You set the shutter speed and the camera sets the aperture based on metering info and current ISO.

M (Manual): You set ISO, shutter speed, and aperture.

B (Bulb/Time): Used for long exposures.

C1 – C5 (Custom Shooting Modes): Used to store user settings that are easily retrieved. Default settings are: C1 – OM-Cinema1 and C2 – OM-Cinema2 (with C3, C4, and C5 empty).

METERING MODES

Menu > Shooting1 > Metering > Metering, or use the super control panel and select Metering.

Digital ESP Metering: The camera divides the scene into 324 areas and tries to determine the best exposure by taking the nature of the scene into consideration. Works well for most scenes, including backlit subjects.

Center Weighted Averaging Metering: The camera looks at the whole scene but gives more emphasis to the area in the center.

Spot Metering: The camera uses a small area (approximately 2% of the frame) to determine exposure.

Spot Metering (Highlight): The camera uses a small area to determine exposure but works to keep bright subjects appearing bright.

Spot Metering (Shadow): The camera uses a small area to determine exposure but works to keep dark subjects appearing dark.

EXPOSURE COMPENSATION

When using P, A, or S Shooting mode, rotate the front dial to adjust the exposure from –5 to +5 stops. Or you can press the Fn button and use the left or right arrow pad buttons. When using M (Manual) shooting mode, Auto ISO must be used in order to enable exposure compensation. Then, press the Fn button and rotate the front or rear dial to adjust the exposure compensation.

To reset exposure compensation, press and hold the OK button.

FOCUS MODES

Menu > AF > 1. AF > Image AF Mode

Menu > AF > 5. AF > Movie AF Mode

S-AF (Single AF): The camera focuses once when the shutter button is pressed halfway down. Best used for static subjects.

C-AF (Continuous AF): The camera starts to focus when the shutter button (or the AF-ON button) is pressed halfway down and continues to focus until the photo is taken.

MF (Manual Focus): Focus is achieved by rotating the focus ring on the lens.

S-AF MF: The camera focuses using single AF, but you can adjust the focus by using the manual focus ring on the lens.

C-AF + TR (Continuous AF + Tracking): The camera starts to focus when the shutter button (or AF-ON button) is pressed halfway down and will try to track the subject until the photo is taken. This cannot be used with: keystone compensation, High Res Shot, focus stacking, focus bracketing, interval timer, HDR, Live ND Shooting, Live GND Shooting, or fisheye compensation.

PreMF (Preset Manual Focus): The camera automatically focuses on the preset focus point when shooting.

[*]AF (Starry Sky AF): Use to photograph pictures of stars in the night sky (see Chapter 04).

[·⁞·] AUTOFOCUS TARGET MODES

Press the arrow keypad buttons to view and move the AF target. You can rotate the front dial to select the size and shape of the focus target.

All Targets: The camera picks which focus target to use from all the targets: 1053 in a 39 x 27 grid for still photos or 741 in a 39 x 19 grid for movies.

Single Target: The camera uses a single focus target.

Small Target: Select a small group of targets, and the camera picks the individual target to use.

Cross: Uses a group of focus targets arranged in a cross formation. The camera picks which of the focus targets to use from the group.

Middle: Uses a middle-sized group of targets arranged in a square. The camera picks which of the focus targets to use.

Large: Uses a large-sized group of targets arranged in a square. The camera picks which of the focus targets to use.

C1-C4 Custom Target: You can create custom focus target sizes and the distance it moves each time.

Note: Menu > AF > 6. AF Target Settings & Operations > AF Target Mode Settings allows you to show which modes are available and set the size and step for C1-C4.

DRIVE MODES

Menu > Shooting1 > 7. Drive Mode > Drive Mode Sequential/Self Timer

Or, on the super control panel, select Drive (sequential/ Self Timer).

Single Frame: The camera takes a single frame each time the shutter button is pressed all the way down.

Sequential: The camera takes up to 20 fps while the shutter release button is held down.

High-Speed Sequential SH1: The camera takes up to 120 fps while the shutter release button is held down. The focus, exposure, and white balance are locked at the values for the first shot for the sequence.

High-Speed Sequential SH2: The camera takes up to 50 fps while the shutter release button is held down. The focus and exposure will be adjusted between every shot when the AF mode is set to C-AF, CA-AF MF, C-AF+TR, or C-AF+TR MF. When Metering during sequence is set to yes (Menu > Camera Settings 1 > Metering > Metering during sequence), the camera will adjust the exposure between each shot.

Pro Capture: Capture starts when the shutter button is pressed halfway down until the button is pressed all the way down. Allows photos to be taken with no shutter lag (see Chapter 04).

12 Sec Self-Timer: The camera takes a photo 12 seconds after the shutter release button is pressed all the way down. The self-timer lamp will illuminate for the first ten seconds and flash for the last two. The focus is achieved when the shutter release button is pressed halfway down.

2 Sec Self-Timer: The camera takes a photo two seconds after the shutter release button is pressed all the way down. The self-timer lamp will flash for the two seconds. The focus is achieved when the shutter release button is pressed halfway down.

Custom Self-Timer: You can determine the self-timer delay and the number of shots taken when the timer expires.

Note: Choose Menu > Shooting1 > 7. Drive Mode > Sequential Shooting Settings to adjust the shooting speed and visibility of the drive modes.

WHITE BALANCE

Press the OK button to open the super control panel, use the arrow keypad to navigate to WB, and use the front dial to select a white balance setting.

AUTO is the setting best suited for most situations. You can use specific preset white balance settings (Daylight, Shade, Cloudy, etc.) when shooting under specific lighting conditions, or you can create a custom white balance using the one-touch white balance feature (see Chapter 04).

IMAGE SIZE/QUALITY

Press the OK button to open the super control panel, use the arrow keypad to select the Image Quality icon, and use the front dial to select the desired setting.

LSF: 5184 x 3888 SuperFine Compression JPEG

LF: 5184 x 3888 Fine Compression JPEG

LN: 5184 x 3888 Normal Compression JPEG

M1N: 3200 x 2400 Normal Compression JPEG

RAW: 5184 x 3888 Lossless Compression ORF

RAW + JPEG: ORF + JPEG

04 OTHER HELPFUL SETTINGS

CREATIVE DIAL

Change the mode by rotating the Creative Dial on the front of the camera.

MONO (Monochrome Profile Control): There are four profiles:

- MONO1 is the standard preset
- MONO2 is a monochrome film look
- MONO3 is an infrared film look
- MONO4 is a softer, reduced-contrast look

COLOR (Color Profile Control): There are four profiles:

- COLOR1 is the standard preset
- COLOR2 has a rich and deep tone
- COLOR3 creates a film-like effect with high saturation
- COLOR4 has a light and soft color tone

| (Picture Mode): See next section.

ART (Art Filter): These modes allow for creative presets and filters to be used. Art modes include Pop Art, Soft Focus, Pale & Light Color, Light Tone, Grainy Film, Pin Hole, Diorama, Cross Process, Gentle Sepia, Dramatic Tone, Key Line, Watercolor, Vintage, Partial Color, Bleach Bypass, and Instant Film.

CRT (Color Creator): The color of the entire image can be set using a combination of 30 levels of hue (rotate the front dial) and 8 levels of saturation (rotate the rear dial).

PICTURE MODES

Open the super control panel and select Picture Mode.

i-Enhance: Camera adjusts the colors and contrast for best results automatically.

Vivid: Choose to capture vivid colors.

Natural: Use for a natural-looking colors.

Muted: Best for images that will be retouched later.

Portrait: Use for photos of people. Enhances skin tone.

Monochrome: Records images in monochrome. Can add color filters and/or tinting.

Custom: Adjust a picture mode to create a custom version.

Underwater: Use to preserve colors captured underwater.

Art Filters: These modes allow for creative presets and filters to be used. Art modes include Pop Art, Soft Focus, Pale & Light Color, Light Tone, Grainy Film, Pin Hole, Diorama, Cross Process, Gentle Sepia, Dramatic Tone, Key Line, Watercolor, Vintage, Partial Color, Bleach Bypass, and Instant Film.

COLOR SPACE

Menu > Shooting1 > 2. Picture Mode/WB > Color Space

sRGB: Smaller color space. Best when images are used directly from the camera.

AdobeRGB: Larger color space. Best used when images will be edited with software.

Note: AdobeRGB is not available in HDR or movie mode when an art filter is selected for the picture mode.

ONE-TOUCH WHITE BALANCE

The One-Touch White Balance feature allows you to quickly set a custom white balance by using a white piece of paper (or other white object) in your scene as a white balance reference.

1. Select One-Touch White Balance (1, 2, 3, or 4) on the WB setting screen, then select Set.

2. Aim the camera at a piece of white paper (fill the frame with the paper) and press the INFO button.

3. The One-Touch White Balance screen opens.

4. Select Yes and press the OK button.

AUTO ISO

Open the super control panel by pressing the OK button. Select ISO and choose Auto. This will set the camera to adjust the ISO automatically.

You can set the maximum and standard values by going to Menu > Shooting1 > 3. ISO/Noise Reduction > Image ISO-A Upper/Default.

EXPOSURE BRACKETING

Menu > Shooting2 > Bracketing > AE BKT

Select the desired exposure bracketing settings (e.g., number of shots, bracketing amounts, etc.) from the list, and press OK.

BKT is displayed in green until the photos in the bracketing sequence have been taken. The first shot is at the current exposure followed by the underexposed images and then the overexposed images.

INFORMATION DISPLAY

Press the INFO button while shooting to switch between information screens.

Choose which displays to show at Menu > Playback > 3. Displays > Info Setting. Add or remove the check mark to show or hide the screen.

Image Only: Only the image is displayed.

Basic Information: A minimum amount of information is displayed.

Overall Display: A wide array of information is displayed.

PRO CAPTURE

Menu > Shooting1 > 7. Drive Mode > Drive Mode Sequential/Self Timer, then select Pro Capture.

Pro Capture starts to record images when the shutter button is pressed halfway down, resulting in no shutter lag when you do press the shutter button all the way down to start taking photos.

Pro Capture (ProCap): Use when the distance to the subject will change during shooting. The camera shoots at up to 20 frames per second, and 70 frames can be captured before the shutter is pressed all the way down. If AF is set to C-AF,

CA-AF MF, C-AF+TR, or C-AF+TR MF, the camera will focus before each shot.

Pro Capture SH1: Use when the distance from the subject to the camera isn't going to change. The camera shoots at up to 120 frames per second, and 70 frames can be captured before the shutter is pressed all the way down. The camera will use S-AF for the focus mode when AF is set to C-AF, C-AF+TR, or S-AF MF when the focus mode is set to CA-AF MF or C-AF+TR MF.

Pro Capture SH2: The camera shoots at up to 50 frames per second, and 70 frames can be captured before the shutter is pressed all the way down. If AF is set to C-AF, CA-AF MF, C-AF+TR, or C-AF+TR MF, the camera will focus between each shot.

Note: This feature is only available with certain lenses.

HIGH RES SHOT

Menu > Shooting2 > 1. Computational Modes > High Res Shot

Use the up and down arrow buttons to select High Res Shot, and press OK. Then use the left and right buttons to select between tripod (80M with 10368 x 7776 resolution) and hand-held (50M 8160 x 6120 resolution) modes. You can also adjust

the following settings before pressing Menu to return to the shooting screen, and the High Res Shot icon will be displayed.

High Res Shot Image Quality: Choose the image quality of a high-resolution shot.

12- or 14-bit depth of Raw Images: 14 bit has richer tones and more color information but makes a larger file than those saved with 12 bit.

Waiting Time: Set the time between pressing the shutter button all the way down and the actual time the photo is taken to help reduce camera shake.

Flash Charge Time: How long the camera waits for the flash to recharge.

Use the CP button to turn High Res Shot on or off and use the front and rear dials to set the tripod or handheld settings.

LIVE ND SHOOTING

Menu > Shooting2 > 1. Computational Modes > Live ND Shooting

Use the up and down arrow buttons to turn Live ND Shooting on or off and select the ND Number and LV Simulation.

ND Number choices are: [ND2 (1EV)], [ND4 (2EV)], [ND8 (3EV)], [ND16 (4EV)], [ND32 (5EV)], [ND64 (6EV)].

LV Simulation can be set to on, where it will show the effects of shutter speed on the display, and off, where you see the standard shooting display.

Press Menu to close the Live ND Shooting setting screen and return to the shooting screen. Adjust the shutter speed using the rear dial while previewing the results in the display. The slowest shutter speed available varies with the selected ND filter: **[ND2 (1EV)],** 1/60 sec; **[ND4 (2EV)],** 1/30 sec; **[ND8 (3EV)],** 1/15 sec; **[ND16 (4EV)],** 1/8 sec; **[ND32 (5EV)],** 1/4 sec; **[ND64 (6EV)],** 1/2 sec.

LIVE GND SHOOTING

Menu > Shooting2 > 1. Computational Modes > Live GND Shooting

Use the up and down arrow buttons to turn Live GND Shooting on or off. Select the GND Number and filter type, then turn Filter Auto Rotate on or off.

GND Number: The three options are: [GND2(1EV)], [GND4(2EV)], and [GND8(3EV)].

Filter Type: Sets the range of gradation for the boundaries of the areas that the effect is applied to (the darkest areas) and the areas with no changes in brightness (unaffected areas). [Soft] produces a wider gradation than [Medium];

[Hard] produces a narrower transition than [Medium], which is right in the middle.

STARRY SKY AUTOFOCUS

Menu > AF > 1.AF > Image AF Mode, then select [*]AF (Starry Sky AF)

Compose the image and press the AF-ON button to initiate starry sky autofocus. The camera displays "[Starry Sky AF is Running]" and the in-focus indicator will be displayed for two seconds once focus is achieved. If focus cannot be achieved, the in-focus indicator will flash. Press the shutter button all the way down to take the photo.

WIRELESS COMMUNICATION

Pair your camera and smartphone to import and edit photos, use your smartphone as a remote control, and more.

1. Launch the OM Image Share app on your smartphone.
2. Open the super control panel and tap on the Wi-Fi/ Bluetooth icon.
3. Select Device Connection and press OK.
4. Follow the on-screen instructions to adjust the Wi-Fi/ Bluetooth settings.

5. Tap the Camera icon at the bottom of the OM Image Share display.

6. Follow the on-screen instructions in the OM Image Share app to scan the QR code and adjust the settings.

RESET CAMERA

Menu > setup > 6. Reset/Clock/Language/Other > Reset/ Initialize Settings

1. Select Reset Shooting Settings to reset only the photography related settings.

2. Select Initialize All Settings to reset everything other than the clock and the language.

05 STEP-BY-STEP SHOOTING INSTRUCTIONS

MULTIPLE EXPOSURES

Create in-camera multiple exposures from two frames:

1. Go to Menu > Shooting2 > 1. Computational Modes > Multiple Exposure.
2. Select Multiple Exposure and press OK, then select either On or Off.
3. Use the arrow keypad to select from the following:

   Auto Gain: [Off] or [On]. [On] cuts the brightness of each frame in half.

   Overlay: [Off] means you want to create the multiple exposure from the next two pictures you take. [On] means you want to shoot a multiple exposure that includes a RAW image that's already on your memory card. If you select On, you'll be prompted to select an image.
4. Press Menu to close the Multiple Exposure settings menu and return to the shooting screen.
5. Take photos for the multiple exposure.

INTERVAL TIMER SHOOTING/ TIME-LAPSE MOVIES

Set the camera to take a series of photos over a period of time or create a time-lapse movie:

1. Go to Menu > Shooting2 > 2. Other Shooting functions > Interval Shooting. Press the OK button.
2. Use the up and down arrow buttons to select On, then press the OK button.
3. Configure the Interval Shooting options:

   Number of Frames: Number of frames to shoot [002] – [9999]

   Start Waiting Time: How long before starting [00:00:00] – [24:00:00].

   Interval Length: How long between each shot [00:00:01] – [24:00:00].

   Interval Mode: Chose priority between interval time [Time Priority] or the number of frames [Frames Priority].

   Exposure Smoothing: Choose to smooth the exposure setting for all frames. The change of exposure will be smooth in time-lapse movie [Off]/[On].

   Time Lapse Movie: [On] saves the individual frames and creates movie. Choose [Off] to save individual photos.

Movie Settings: Choose frame size ([4K] or [FullHD]) and frame rate ([30fps], [15fps], [10fps], or [5fps]) if creating movies.

4. Press the Menu button to exit the menu.
5. Take photos.

HDR HDR

Combine multiple images to reduce the contrast and improve tonal range:

1. Go to Menu > Shooting2 > 1. Computational Modes > HDR.
2. Select from the following options, then press OK.

   HDR1 and HDR2: Automatic modes that create a single in-camera HDR image. HDR1 is more natural looking; HDR2 is a more processed and painterly look.

   3f 2.0EV–5f 3.0EV: To bracket a series of exposures so that you can create an HDR image yourself with post-processing software, select one of these five combinations of number of frames along with the amount of exposure change between shots.
3. Take photos.

06 TYPICAL SHOOTING SCENARIOS

Shooting Scenario

PORTRAIT

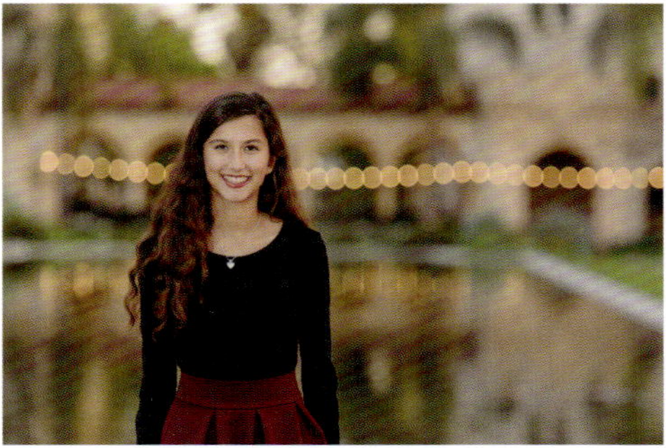

KEY PRINCIPLES

- The key to a portrait like this is shallow depth of field. Shoot in **APERTURE PRIORITY** mode and set the aperture to the lowest aperture your lens offers (such as **f/2.8** or **f/4**).
- Remember to **focus on the eyes**.

- If the image is too dark or too light, use **EXPOSURE COMPENSATION** to adjust the brightness level.
- If the image is blurry from a slow shutter speed, **raise the ISO** to increase your sensor's sensitivity to light, thus allowing for a faster shutter speed.
- Remember to use a **focal length of 50mm or greater** so that you don't distort your subject's face.

SHOOTING SCENARIO
GROUP PORTRAIT

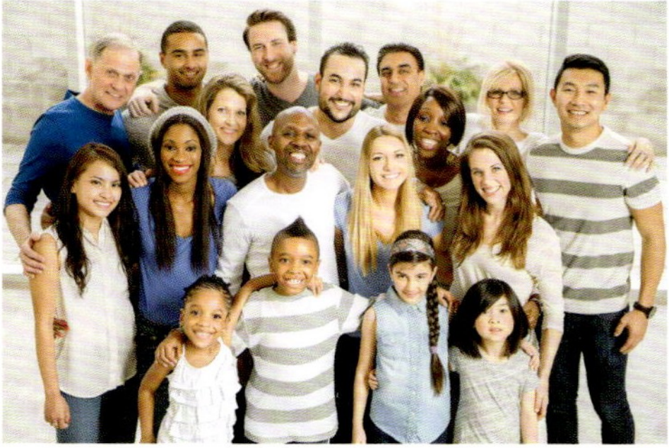

KEY PRINCIPLES

- In order to get everyone in focus, you need a deep depth of field. Shoot in **APERTURE PRIORITY** mode and set the aperture between **f/8–f/16 for a deeper depth of field**.
- **Focus on the person in the middle of the group.** Check focus by zooming in to view it at 100% and checking the faces in the group. If anyone is out of focus, use a smaller aperture for deeper depth of field.
- Use **DIGITAL ESP METERING** mode to account for the light in the entire scene.
- **Arrange the group so they can all see you** (and you can see them).
- Use **EXPOSURE COMPENSATION** if the image is too bright or too dark.
- If the image is blurry, **raise the ISO** to allow the camera to use a faster shutter speed.

SHOOTING SCENARIO

LANDSCAPE

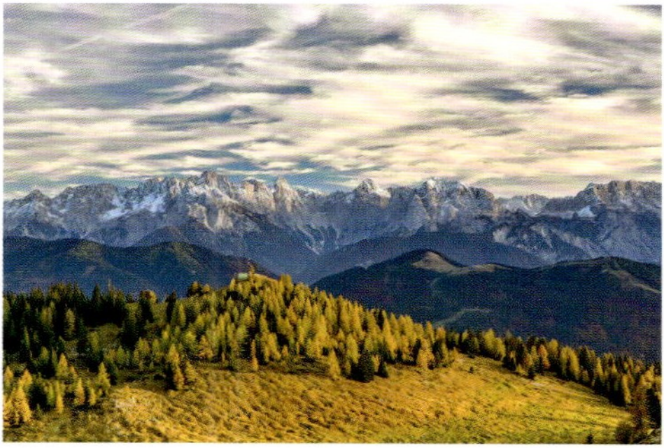

KEY PRINCIPLES

- Shoot in **APERTURE PRIORITY** to control depth of field. Start with **f/16** to ensure deep depth of field.
- **Use a tripod** to eliminate camera movement. Whenever your camera is on a tripod, also make sure **IMAGE STABILIZATION** is turned off.
- Use **DIGITAL ESP METERING** mode and **SINGLE AUTOFOCUS (S-AF)**.
- **Set the ISO to a low setting (LOW–200)** to avoid any digital noise.

- Shoot in **RAW** so that you have the most available information when editing later.
- Consider **BRACKETING** your exposures.

SHOOTING SCENARIO
FREEZE ACTION

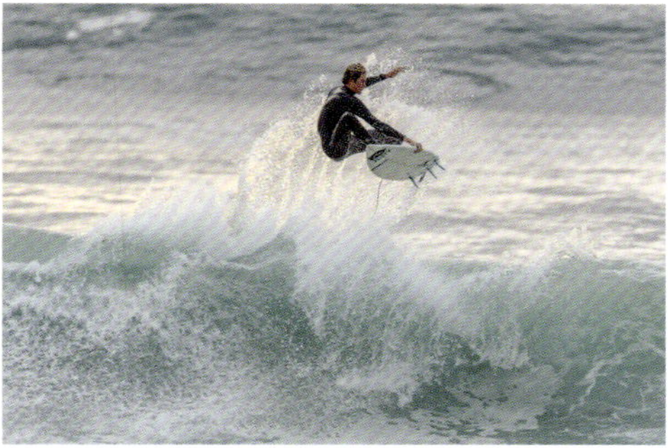

KEY PRINCIPLES

- Use **SHUTTER PRIORITY** mode and set the shutter speed to a value that will freeze the action. The appropriate shutter speed depends on your subject and its movement, but it could be anywhere between **1/500–1/8000 sec**.

- Use **CONTINUOUS AUTOFOCUS (C-AF)** so that the camera keeps focusing as the subject moves.
- If the image is dark or blurry, **raise the ISO** or try **AUTO ISO** to automatically have the camera adjust the ISO as needed.

SHOOTING SCENARIO

SHOWING MOTION—PANNING

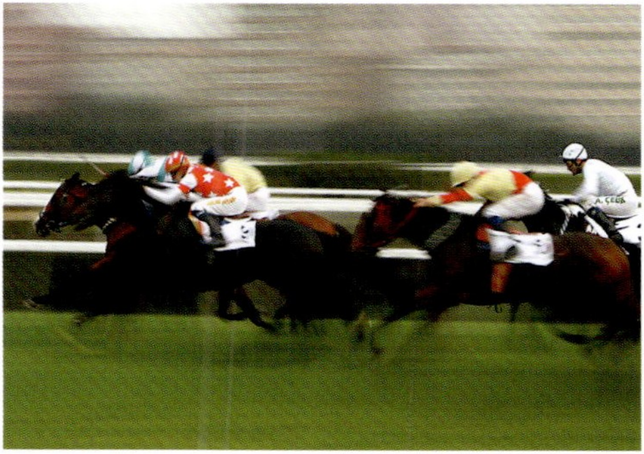

KEY PRINCIPLES

- Shoot in **SHUTTER PRIORITY** mode and set the shutter speed to a value that is slow enough to allow for the subject to move during the exposure.

- **Follow the subject** across the frame as you shoot.
- Try **LIVE VIEW**, which allows you to see the subject during the exposure on the bigger monitor.
- Use **CONTINUOUS AF + TRACKING (C-AF+TR)** so the camera will continue to track the subject as you're panning.

SHOOTING SCENARIO
LOW-LIGHT ACTION

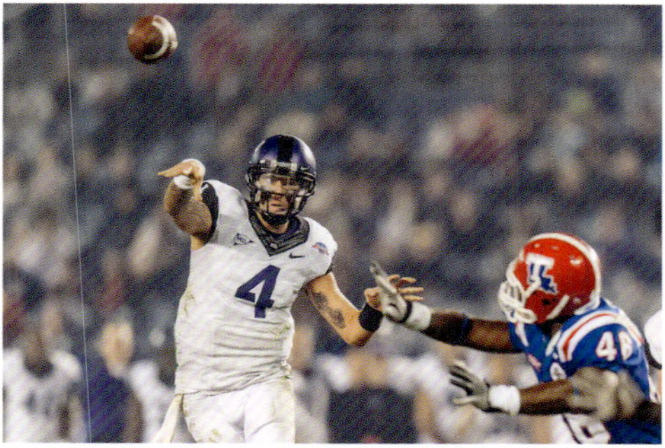

KEY PRINCIPLES

- Shoot in **APERTURE PRIORITY** mode and use a wide aperture such as **f/2.8** or **f/4**.

- Use **SPOT METERING**, and meter on the subject's face.
- Use **CONTINUOUS AUTOFOCUS (C-AF)** and a **SINGLE AF TARGET**.
- **Set the ISO to 1600 or higher**, depending on the amount of available light.
- If the image is blurry, **increase the ISO** to allow for a faster shutter speed.

SHOOTING SCENARIO
LONG EXPOSURE

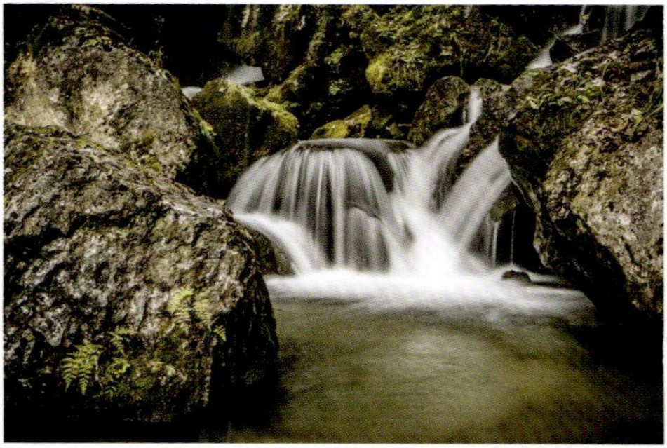

KEY PRINCIPLES

- Shoot either in **BULB** mode, where the shutter stays open as long as the shutter button is pressed, or **LIVE TIME** mode, where you press the shutter button once to open the shutter and press it again to end the exposure.
- **Use a tripod** to keep the camera stable. **Turn off IMAGE STABILIZATION.**
- Use the **SINGLE AUTOFOCUS (S-AF)** mode, or try **manual focus** if the camera is having a hard time locking on focus.
- **Use a low ISO** (80–400) and **shoot RAW** to ensure a high-quality file.
- For night sky photos, try the **[*] STARRY SKY AUTOFOCUS** mode.

SHOOTING SCENARIO

MACRO/CLOSE-UP

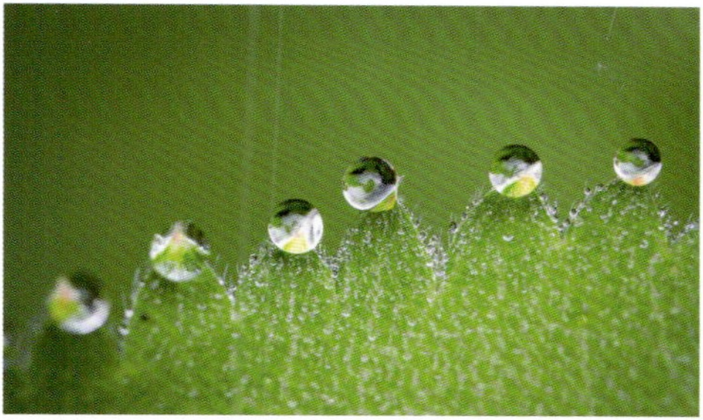

KEY PRINCIPLES

- Shoot in **APERTURE PRIORITY** mode, and **use a small aperture** to ensure you achieve enough depth of field (this image was shot at f/13).
- Use **DIGITAL ESP METERING** to analyze the light in the entire frame.
- A **tripod** is very useful for keeping the camera steady.
- Use **MANUAL FOCUS**, and **zoom in** to confirm your focus is tack sharp.
- Try using a dedicated **macro lens or close-up filters** to make sure you can achieve sharp focus when you're so close to the subject.

SHOOTING SCENARIO

VIDEO RECORDING/VLOGGING

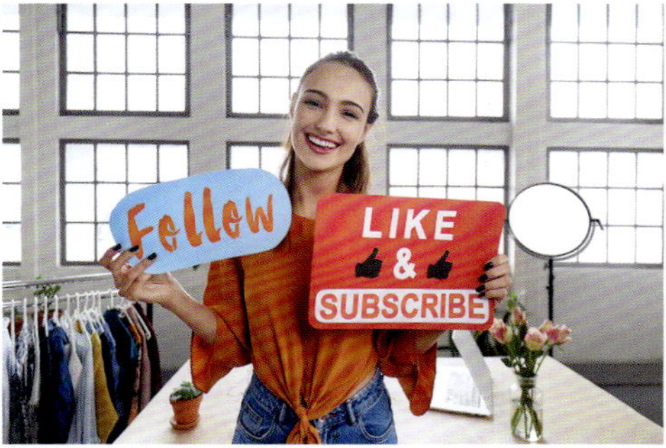

KEY PRINCIPLES

- Use a **shallow depth of field** to keep the viewers' attention on the subject. A **wide aperture** will keep the subject in focus while having the area in front of and behind the subject fall out of focus.
- Use **24 fps** for a more cinematic look.
- Set the **shutter speed to twice the frame rate** or as close as you can get. If using 24 fps, the shutter speed should be 1/50 (or 1/60) second.
- Use an **external microphone** for better sound. The Rode VideoMic GO II is a great starter microphone.

- Keep the camera stable with a **tripod or gimble**. Smooth footage looks more professional.
- Use the **swing-out monitor** to watch the video being recorded. Remember to leave 1 or 2 seconds of nothing at the beginning and end of your video clips—this will make them much easier to edit later.

CANON

EOS 5D MARK IV

POCKET GUIDE